The Useless Cat Alphabet Book

By Janet Jeanes

The Useless Cat Alphabet Book

Janet Jeanes

This edition published in 2016

First published in 2012
By Wakkajak Publishers New Zealand

Copyright © 2012 Janet Jeanes
Text, Illustrations and Design by Janet Jeanes

The moral right of the author and illustrator, Janet Jeanes has been asserted.

All rights reserved, without limiting the rights under copyright reserved above. No part of this publication may be reproduced, stored or introduced into a retrieval system, or transmitted, in any form or by any means (electronic, mechanical, photocopying, recording or otherwise), without the prior permission of both the copyright owner and publisher of this book.

ISBN 9780473275518

A catalogue record for this book is available from the National Library of New Zealand.

wakkajak.com

For my family

This book is the ideal book for active young minds and bodies - minds that are ready to learn, and bodies that are ready to move. An action ABC book! These bright attractive pages with great illustrations bring learning and physical activity together. Encourage your little ones to do the actions as they learn the alphabet in a fun way.

Bb
balance

Cc
crawl

Ff

flop

Gg
gallop

Hh
hang

Ii
imagine

Mm
move

Rr
run

Ss
stretch

Tt
tumble

Vv
vanish

Ww
wobble

Xx

relax

Yy
yawn

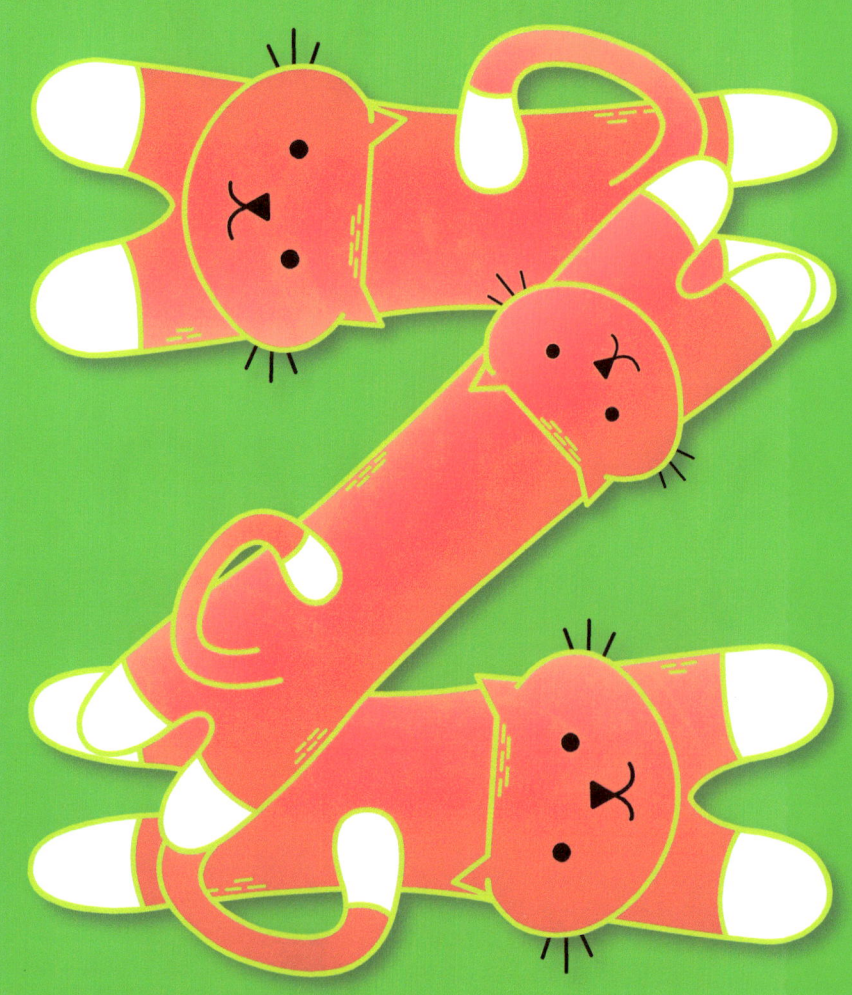

www.ingramcontent.com/pod-product-compliance
Lightning Source LLC
Chambersburg PA
CBHW060756090426
42736CB00002B/49